No two relationships are alike. It would be like comparing two leaves from the same tree. On the surface, they both appear the same, but it's the tiny, undefinable differences that make the two unique.

— Karen Culver
Chicken Soup for the Couple's Soul

*The best minute you spend
is the one you invest
in your family.*

— Ken Blanchard

The human spirit is stronger than anything that can happen to it.

– C. C. Scott

*For all the freedom of life...
I'll take the
responsibility of caring
for the woman
who vowed to love me.*

— Bob Welch
Chicken Soup for the Couple's Soul

*Intimate relationships teach us
when to hold on more tightly,
and when to let go.*

— Jack Canfield and Mark V. Hansen

*If I can stop one heart
from breaking,
I shall not live in vain.*

– Emily Dickinson

I knew marriage took
a lot of hard work.
I never had the expectation it'd
be sweet and wonderful.
If we were going to grow and change,
we'd have to make an effort.

— Jann Mitchell
Chicken Soup for the Couple's Soul

Baby You Are...
my shining light,
my day and night...

– David L. Weatherford
Chicken Soup for the Couple's Soul

Your heart is not living until it has experienced pain.... The pain of love breaks open the heart, even if it is as hard as a rock.

— Hazart Inayat Khan

If love does not know how to give and take without restrictions, it is not love, but a transaction.

— Emma Goldman

Remember the day you fell
in love—and recreate it.
Hold hands.
Say "I love you" with your eyes.

— Mark and Chrissy Donnelly
Chicken Soup for the Couple's Soul

*Kindness is a language.
We all understand it.*

— Diana Chapman
Chicken Soup for the Couple's Soul

Inside our oldest commitments can lie our newest celebrations.

— Maggie Bedrosian
Chicken Soup for the Couple's Soul

Start each day with a hug.
Serve breakfast in bed.
Say "I love you" every time you part ways.

– Mark and Chrissy Donnelly
Chicken Soup for the Couple's Soul

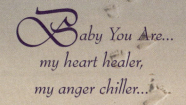

Baby You Are...
my heart healer,
my anger chiller...

— David L. Weatherford
Chicken Soup for the Couple's Soul

There are moments when love can be experienced as quite ordinary, expressed in a simple smile of acceptance from your beloved.

— Jack Canfield and Mark V. Hansen

I hope to be a grandfather who can slow dance with his wife, knowing that indeed, there is no greater blessing than love.

— Justin R. Haskin
Chicken Soup for the Couple's Soul

Blessed is the influence of one true, loving human soul on another.

– George Eliot

Those who have never known the deep intimacy and hence the companionship of happy mutual love have missed the best thing that life has to give.

– Bertrand Russell

It was a hug that said "you're not alone." It was a hug that, just when I thought all my strength was used up, and I couldn't go on, renewed me.

— Ann W. Compton
Chicken Soup for the Couple's Soul

*Love doesn't just sit there,
like a stone;
it has to be made,
like bread,
remade all the time,
made new.*

— Ursula K. Le Guin

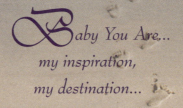

Baby You Are...
my inspiration,
my destination...

— David L. Weatherford
Chicken Soup for the Couple's Soul

The great doing of little things makes the great life.

— Eugenia Price

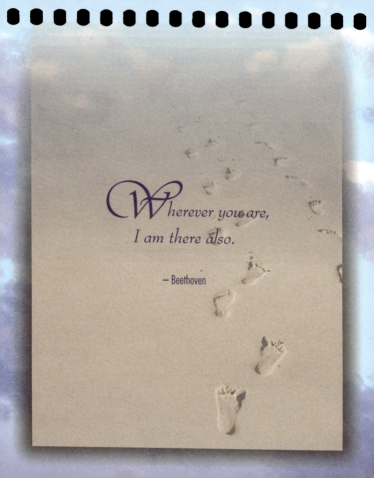

The best times of my life are the times we spend together, whether sitting quietly watching television or enjoying an afternoon at a...game.

— David A. Manzi
Chicken Soup for the Couple's Soul

She is my wife,
my lover,
my best friend.

– David A. Manzi
Chicken Soup for the Couple's Soul

Sharing a day's details by phone is never as good as sharing a day. Side by side, life happens to you simultaneously. You carry the same memories, whose details blend each time you retell them.

— Susan Ager
Chicken Soup for the Couple's Soul

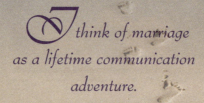

I think of marriage as a lifetime communication adventure.

— Maggie Bedrosian
Chicken Soup for the Couple's Soul

Be your partner's biggest fan.
Give the love your partner
wants to receive.
Give the love you want to receive.

— Mark and Chrissy Donnelly
Chicken Soup for the Couple's Soul

We discovered no
disagreement is so small
it can't evolve into a major problem,
and...two monologues
do not equal a dialogue.

— Nick Harrison
Chicken Soup for the Couple's Soul

*I believe love is
a personal thing;
it can best be valued by
the person you give it to.*

– Karen Culver
Chicken Soup for the Couple's Soul

To love is to place our happiness in the happiness of another.

— Gottfried Wilhelm Van Lubreitz

As long as one can
admire and love,
then one is young forever.

– Pablo Casals

Apologize sincerely.

Be forgiving.

— Mark and Chrissy Donnelly
Chicken Soup for the Couple's Soul

In the eyes of the soul of my husband...I am still, and will always be,...eighteen, as carefree and whimsical as the day we met.

– Shari Cohen
Chicken Soup for the Couple's Soul

In marriage, there is no scorecard. You do little things for each other to make the other's life easier. If you think of it as helping the person you love, you don't become annoyed with doing...any task, because you're doing it out of love.

— Marguerite Murer
Chicken Soup for the Couple's Soul

The applause of a single human being is of great consequence.

– Samuel Johnson

God is in the details.

– Ludwig Mies van der Rohe

Baby You Are...

my pain reliever,

my spring fever...

– David L. Weatherford
Chicken Soup for the Couple's Soul

One word frees us of all the weight and pain of life: The word is "love."

— Sophocles

*There is no miracle
greater than love.
It is God's most precious
gift to us.*

— Jack Canfield and Mark V. Hansen

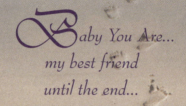

*Baby You Are...
my best friend
until the end...*

— David L. Weatherford
Chicken Soup for the Couple's Soul

We were sharing something new. A walk, a sweet, safe, comfortable companionship that offered new love each day, and a kiss that had never happened before and would never happen again. This moment was new, as each moment always would be.

— Maggie Bedrosian
Chicken Soup for the Couple's Soul

Whoso loves, believes the impossible.

— Elizabeth Barrett Browning

Let her cry in your arms.
Tell him you understand.
Laugh at his jokes.

— Mark and Chrissy Donnelly
Chicken Soup for the Couple's Soul

*Intimate relationships
teach us to be compassionate,
caring, and forgiving.*

— Jack Canfield and Mark V. Hansen

*Flowers grow
out of dark moments.*

— Corita Kent

Funny: When you're young, you say, "Life is short" to justify your excursions, geographic or emotional. When you're older, you say the same thing to justify staying home with the one you love.

— Susan Ager
Chicken Soup for the Couple's Soul

Marriage...has its ups and downs; some days are simply down days and not a reason to leave.

– Jann Mitchell
Chicken Soup for the Couple's Soul

*There is nothing you can do,
achieve, or buy that will
outshine the peace,
joy, and happiness of being
in communion with the partner
you love.*

— Drs. Evelyn and Paul Moschetta
Chicken Soup for the Couple's Soul

*Now join your hands,
and with your hands,
your hearts.*

— Shakespeare

*Where love reigns
the impossible may be attained.*

— Indian Proverb

You are not alone in your troubles. I promised to stand beside you through everything life brought our way.

— Roxanne Willems Snopek
Chicken Soup for the Couple's Soul

*Never go to bed mad.
Put your partner first
in your prayers.*

— Mark and Chrissy Donnelly
Chicken Soup for the Couple's Soul

Sweetheart, you're still the most important person in the world to me.

— Ann W. Compton
Chicken Soup for the Couple's Soul

My lifetime listens to yours.

— Muriel Ruckeyser

I can honestly state that after all this time together, my love for [my wife] has not diminished in the slightest way. In fact, through each passing day, I find myself more and more enraptured by her beauty.

– David A. Manzi
Chicken Soup for the Couple's Soul

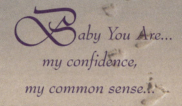

Baby You Are...
my confidence,
my common sense...

– David L. Weatherford
Chicken Soup for the Couple's Soul

Although the form of a relationship may change, the love doesn't ever have to die.

— Bonnie Furman
Chicken Soup for the Couple's Soul

The only genuine love worthy of a name is unconditional.

— John Powell

*Life is a dance,
a movement of rhythms,
directions, stumbles, missteps,
at times slow and precise,
or fast and wild and joyous.*

— Thelda Bevens
Chicken Soup for the Couple's Soul

We are convinced that we are true soul mates. When I was fifteen and praying for my future wife, she was fourteen and prying for her future husband.

— Don Buehner
Chicken Soup for the Couple's Soul

I may have all knowledge and understand all secrets; I may have all the faith needed to move mountains — but if I have no love, I am nothing.

— 1 Corinthians 13:2

Even in the bleakest times, there are gifts to be discovered.

— Jann Mitchell
Chicken Soup for the Couple's Soul

Appreciate her inner beauty.
Do the other person's
chores for a day.
Encourage wonderful dreams.

— Mark and Chrissy Donnelly
Chicken Soup for the Couple's Soul

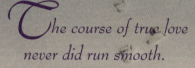

The course of true love never did run smooth.

— Shakespeare,
A Midsummer Night's Dream

The one thing we can never get
enough of is love.
And the one thing we never give
enough of is love.

– Henry Miller

Baby You Are...
my sweetest gift,
my emotional lift...

— David L. Weatherford
Chicken Soup for the Couple's Soul

We would always kiss good night, and that made everything better.

— Laura Lagana
Chicken Soup for the Couple's Soul

*Nothing in this world is more
powerful than love.
Not money, greed, hate, or passion.
Words cannot describe it.
Poets and writers try.
They can't because it is different
for each of us.*

– Justin R. Haskin
Chicken Soup for the Couple's Soul

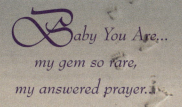

Baby You Are...

my gem so rare,

my answered prayer...

– David L. Weatherford
Chicken Soup for the Couple's Soul

There is no surprise more magical than the surprise of being loved; it is God's finger on man's shoulder.

– Charles Morgan

What might seem like an odd union to you or me is perfectly ordinary to the couple involved.

– Karen Culver
Chicken Soup for the Couple's Soul

Write unexpected love letters.
Go on a date once every week.

— Mark and Chrissy Donnelly
Chicken Soup for the Couple's Soul

I have sought to come near you, I have called to you with all my heart; and when I went out toward you I found you coming toward me.

— Judah Halevi

Sometimes love reveals itself in the unmatched level of understanding and friendship we share with our mate and no one else.

— Jack Canfield and Mark V. Hansen

*Compliment freely and often.
Appreciate—and celebrate—
your differences.
Live each day as if it's your last.*

– Mark and Chrissy Donnelly
Chicken Soup for the Couple's Soul

I will always be grateful for the priceless gift he gave me: the wisdom to know that all our experiences in life make us not less valuable, but more valuable, not less able to love, but more able to love.

—Joanna Slan
Chicken Soup for the Couple's Soul

$\mathcal{A}$cross the years,
I will walk with you—
in deep, green forests;
on shores of sand;
and when our time
on earth is through
in heaven, too,
you will have
my hand.

— Robert Sexton
Chicken Soup for the Couple's Soul

*Love cures people,
both the ones who give it,
and the ones who receive it.*

– Karl Menninger

I remembered the excitement of meeting someone you didn't know anything about and slowly discovering all the adorable details of his personality; the joy of finding out what you had in common; the first date, the first touch, the first kiss, the first snuggle, the first everything.

— Maggie Bedrosian
Chicken Soup for the Couple's Soul

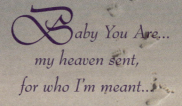

*Baby You Are...
my heaven sent,
for who I'm meant...*

— David L. Weatherford
Chicken Soup for the Couple's Soul

The most important feature of our relationship is that it has never lost the sense of romance that bloomed when we first met. Too often marriage kills the romance that was born in the courtship of a relationship.

– David A. Manzi
Chicken Soup for the Couple's Soul

I want to thank you....
The hug you gave me was
exactly what I needed.

— Ann W. Compton
Chicken Soup for the Couple's Soul

Baby You Are...
my heart and soul,
my life made whole...

— David L. Weatherford
Chicken Soup for the Couple's Soul

Two are better than one....
If one falls down, his friend
can help him up.
But pity the man who falls and
has no one to help him up.

— Ecclesiastes 4:9,10

Relationships are about what you put in and what you take out. And the only people who can judge the worth of what they receive are the people in the commitment.

— Karen Culver
Chicken Soup for the Couple's Soul

There's something special about families...a home of your own. The peace of mind that comes from doing the right thing.

— Justin R. Haskin
Chicken Soup for the Couple's Soul

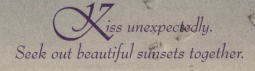

*Kiss unexpectedly.
Seek out beautiful sunsets together.*

– Mark and Chrissy Donnelly
Chicken Soup for the Couple's Soul

*W*alk barefoot on the beach together. Ask her to marry you again. Say yes.

— Mark and Chrissy Donnelly
Chicken Soup for the Couple's Soul

Appreciate that time changes people, and…encourage each other to grow.

— Jann Mitchell
Chicken Soup for the Couple's Soul

What comes from the heart, touches the heart.

— Don Sibet

Baby You Are...
my source of laughter,

my everafter.

– David L. Weatherford
Chicken Soup for the Couple's Soul

Love is the most powerful, magical force in the universe, and there is nowhere it displays its beauty and wonder more than in the intimate relationship between two people.

—Jack Canfield and Mark V. Hansen

A Little Spoonful of
Chicken Soup for the Couple's Soul™

Copyright © 1999 Canfield, Hansen, Donnelly, Donnelly
and De Angelis
All Rights Reserved.

Published by Blessings Unlimited, Pentagon Towers
P.O. Box 398004, Edina, MN 55439

All rights reserved. No part of this book may be
reproduced in any form without permission
in writing from the publisher.

Design by Lecy Design

ISBN 1-58375-550-0

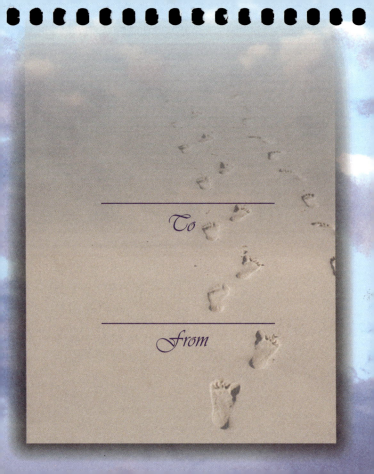